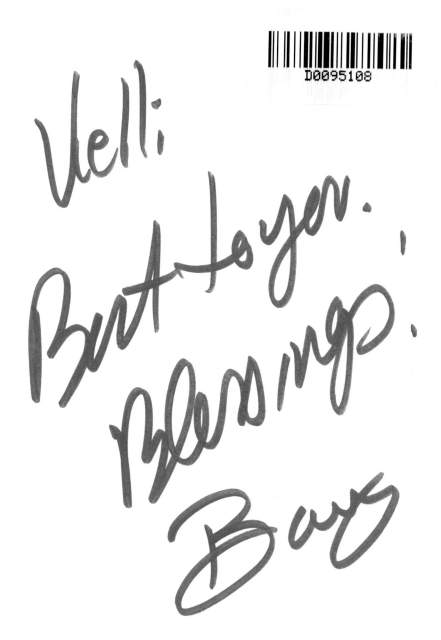

Velli

But to you.

Blessings'

Barys

Barry Spencer teaches from his own experience that earning money is just the first step. Too few wealthy people ask the bigger questions: how do I ensure that my wealth endures and is used wisely to fulfill my wishes while I'm living and transferred to my children, grandchildren and beyond. As the co-founder of a family business who has taken these steps, I can highly recommend this book.

—Rich DeVos, co-founder of Amway,
owner of NBA Orlando Magic

If you're serious about your financial future then read and absorb the message in this brilliant book by my friend Barry Spencer. Barry truly cares about your success!

—James Malinchak, featured on ABCs Hit TV show, "Secret Millionaire", and author of, *Millionaire Entrepreneur Secrets* and founder of, www.BigMoneySpeaker.com

This book will impact lives and bring peace and enrichment into the lives of those who have the blessings of reading it. For the wealthy it gives them a wonderful canvas to begin painting their legacy upon.

—Wally Armstrong, former touring golf professional, author of *The Mulligan*

If you've acquired significant wealth and want to see it endure - for the benefit of you, your family, and your community, then Barry Spencer's latest book is a must read. Enjoy it. More importantly, put it into action!

—Scott Keffer, CEO, The Scott Keffer Companies author of *Giving Transforms You!*

Barry Spencer covers many of the deeply intimate and essential non-technical questions that need to be asked - but all too often are not – by estate and business planning clients – and by their counselors. This book covers some of the most important "people planning" reasons to engage in estate planning."

—Stephan R. Leimberg, CEO of Leimberg and LeClair, Inc. creator of The Tools and Techniques of Estate Planning, and co-author of *Tax Planning With Life Insurance*.

This book contains the wisdom of a family who has been there and done that. A book written from real world experience with sizable family wealth.

—Keith Thomson, author of *What Was Your Greatgrandmother's Name?*

As a growing nonprofit we depend on our loyal donors for their faithful support. Legacy gifts and planned giving is so very critical to sustain our mission. I wish all our donors could read this informative practical book.

—Tim Marks, President & COO,
Metropolitan Ministries, Tampa, Florida

Barry Spencer is a man who has both a heart and a passion to help affluent families navigate the choppy and sometimes even stormy seas faced by those who possess surplus material wealth. This book will give you a sense of both his heart and his process for assisting families to be both thoughtful and strategic in what they choose to do with all that they have. If you want to experience maximum personal and financial impact with all you possess, this book will set you on that path. I can be certain you will indeed enjoy the journey.

—E.G. "Jay" Link, President Kardia, Inc.
& Stewardship Ministries

This book offers wealthy families insights into the impact their wealth can have in the community today, while preserving the family legacy. I highly recommend it to you.

—Bryan Green, President & CEO,
Helping Hands Ministries

I knew the man who Barry describes as godly, successful, thoughtful, conscientious, and caring. Indeed, his father was all of these. At the heart of this book is a potential if unleashed can transform treasure into tools and a plan into plenty for the gospel, the nations, and the kingdom of God. Wealth can be enjoyed, employed, and enduring. But it can also be divisive, damaging, and disrupting. No wonder Jesus said, "What shall it profit a man if he gains the whole world, and loses his own soul?"

—Ken Whitten, Senior Pastor
Idlewild Baptist Church, Tampa, Florida

A Message from My Mother

Had my husband known before he died what we know today about what has transpired with our wealth, he would have done what my son talks about in this book. Even more, he would recommend all his friends, who care about their spouse, family and charitable causes, to do the same. Now with the wealth I have left to manage I have taken these steps in my planning and have the peace of mind and confidence about what I'm doing with my wealth now and what will happen with it when I'm gone.

—G. Yvonne Spencer

Spencer/Murphey

The Secret of
Wealth With No Regrets

Barry H Spencer

with Cecil Murphey

Boomfish Press

ISBN 10-0615848931
ISBN 13-9780615848938

Boomfish Press

www.TheSecretofWealthWithNoRegrets.com

Part 1:

Gaining a Wealth With No Regrets Mindset

Getting different results requires
a different way of thinking
about your wealth.

Wealth With No Regrets is founded on wisdom and knowledge.

I have riches and honor, as well as

lasting wealth . . .

—Solomon

1. Why I Wrote This Book

Anyone would have called my father a success—and he was. A self-made millionaire by age 30, he had become a multimillionaire long before he died at age 62. Despite obstacles and a few missteps along the way, like all successful entrepreneurs he was resilient and persistent and died far richer than he had ever dreamed.

I was at his bedside most of the last four months of his life. He asked only one thing. "Whatever you do, be sure you take care of your mother."

I've tried to honor his last request, but it hasn't been easy. My father didn't realize it, but he failed to put in place all he could to ensure that my mother, his estate, and ultimately his legacy, would be preserved.

No one shared with him the secret to having wealth without regrets.

"I don't have any estate tax due," too many say, "because I can pass my riches on to my spouse estate tax free."

That sounds good, but it doesn't work. It shifts the responsibility to the spouse to sort through resolving the tax burden and how to ensure no regrets. Delaying the responsibility happens all too often. That's what happened with my father's estate plan. If done correctly, however, there can be *zero* estate taxes due even at the death of the second spouse.

You can have a zero estate-tax plan for you and your spouse regardless of the changes in tax laws.

Imagine you have been handed a multi-million dollar business. You don't know anything about the business you have to run.

What questions immediately come to mind?

- What do I do now?
- Where is the business located?
- What does the business own?
- What does the business produce or sell?
- What are the sources of revenue and how does it turn a profit?
- What purposes did I intend for the assets and to whom did I intend them to go?

Sound perplexing?

Imagine that happening to your spouse and heirs. That is exactly what happens because of most estate plans.

When my father died, we were left confused about what he owned and what we were supposed to do. In the midst of our grief over losing a dearly loved man, we scrambled to figure it out. The unintended confusion about the multimillion dollar estate led to family conflict, broken trust, and closed communication.

My father never imagined this would become the problem of his estate and family. He left an 88-page estate plan document.

Shouldn't that have been sufficient?

Six months after Dad's death, his single, unintended failure loomed over our family. Even now, it's still disheartening. The fiasco doesn't represent the thoughtful, conscientious, and caring man that he was. He hired reputable and well-intentioned advisors following their instructions.

But that wasn't enough! He had outgrown their capabilities.

No one told him the secret to living with no regrets. **He simply didn't know there was another way.**

I discovered, to my surprise, that the odds had been stacked against him.

Of the majority of affluent people—those who have a surplus of financial resources—about seven out of ten fail to adequately prepare their estate and set it up for their family to manage the wealth they leave behind.[1]

Our family was among that seven out of ten.

After exhaustive research and extensive training in the area of estate planning, I finally figured out the mistakes that were made. That understanding made me determine to help other affluent families avoid experiencing the same failure. There is another way.

I wrote this book because I want you to know the secret to wealth with no regrets.

You can be among the exclusive three out of ten affluent families who succeed in their wealth-transfer planning, and live their wealth today with no regrets.

---

[1] *Preparing Heirs: Five Steps to a Successful Transition of Family Wealth and Values* by Roy Williams and Vic Preisser (Robert Reed Publishers, 2010).

The estate planning professionals are doing their job as they know how to do it. But the statistic remains that seven of ten estates fail in their transfers. Negligence on the part of estate-planning professionals accounts for only 3 percent of those failures.

The results point to the fact that they're limited in their capabilities of resolving the bigger wealth issues.

It's like having the water main line burst in your house and trying to fix it with duct tape. You feel good that you did something, but the water is still leaking and you also know the tape won't last for long. This isn't to speak against professionals who work in the field of estate planning. What they are trained for and capable of doing for you is a start—and often a good start.

It's rarely enough.

To create wealth with no regrets that allows you and generations to follow and flourish requires a different approach to planning, a kind that the three out of ten use.

Give yourself and your family the greatest gift you can leave: An easily understandable written path that ensures wealth with no regrets, which starts with a big envisioned future and knowing exactly the end in mind for you, your family and the impact you desire to have with your wealth.

Establish a written and well thought out plan for more fully enjoying your wealth now and for the generations that follow.

What Now?

1. Do you know with certainty that you have a zero estate-tax plan for you and your spouse?
2. Is there something you want to accomplish with your wealth that goes beyond leaving your assets behind?
3. Do you have an easily understood designed no regrets picture of the future, that captures the desires of your heart in addition to your assets?
4. Have you ensured that you are not passing on the must answer financial and non-financial questions about wealth for your spouse to answer after you're gone?

Wealth With No Regrets is a living plan, not merely a death-preparation plan.

When I stand before God at the end of my life,
I would hope that I would not have a single
bit of talent left, and could say,
"I used everything you gave me."
—Erma Bombeck

2. Why Not a Living Plan?

Attorneys speak a different kind of language than most of us. When your spouse says, "Let's meet with the attorney," you probably don't get excited.

Yet you've been told estate planning happens in the law office around a conference room table. You feel you are there because you have to be, and not because you want to be.

Most of your experiences are customized to you, so why not this one? That is, you sit in first class when you fly, go backstage at the theater, or watch a football game from a reserved section. The maitre d' calls you by name. You receive the favored seats when you appear at the country club. You don't blend in with the crowd; but you stand apart from them.

Why not expect the same treatment when it comes to wealth planning?

Most of the time, however, in that area you're treated like every other person, asked the same questions, and get the same estate plan as anyone else.

You are affluent, which is to say you have more than you need to survive. You have a surplus or abundance of financial resources.

You don't talk about your assets and income, and may not even think of yourself as affluent or wealthy.

Are you among the wealthiest Americans?[2]

10% have a minimum net worth of approximately $800,000.
5% have a minimum net worth of approximately $1.5 million.
1% have a minimum net worth of a approximately $6 million.

You can't take your earthly treasures with you, but you can accomplish extraordinary good right now—while you're alive—and be aware of what comes from sharing your affluence.

Are your advisors helping you develop a living wealth plan? Or are they only helping you with an estate plan that prepares your estate for when you die?

By contrast, a living plan results in having many additional planning options available to you. Once you've decided what you need for yourself, your lifestyle, and your future, there is more you can do.

---

[2] The Affluent Market Tracking Study #19, April 15, 2011, American Affluence Research Center, Inc.

What if:

- you didn't have to pay any gift and estate taxes but could leave more to your heirs and to charity?
- you could plan more wisely for the inheritances you want to distribute and also inspire the next generation to greatness?
- you could—right now—choose to give your tax dollars to charities you care about instead of giving them to Uncle Sam?
- you could build a wealth plan that captures your heart and includes all the available options?
- you could maximize your surplus resources for the greater good of those around you?
- you could provide the basics of food, water, and shelter for other families or even for an entire village?
- you were free to spend more time investing in the family and relationships that matter most to you?
- your philanthropic efforts became a family affair so that generosity becomes a way of life in your family for generations?
- you had more time to do the things that matter most to you. Could you get excited about planning?

Yes, I did write *excited* about planning.

It's not just about what you can do, but about what you want to do.

You can connect your heart to planning options.

That's not only the wisest and best strategy, it's the most satisfying. I encourage you to engage your deepest feelings and desires.

If you start there, you can apply all the available strategies to accomplish what you want to do with the wealth you're blessed to have. It also allows you to employ the right planning techniques.

What could happen today if your deepest emotions and most important relationships drove your wealth planning?

- What might you decide differently if you considered your relationships more carefully and deeply?
- What could you do differently if you factored in your passions and your as-yet-unfulfilled dreams?
- What good could you accomplish if you considered what you are able to do for those you love and for others in society?
- How fulfilled and purposeful would you feel if you were able to use your abundant resources *while you're alive* to fulfill your deepest desires?
- What if you were able to do such things with confidence and assurance right now, and your heirs and the charities you care about would benefit?

Why would you wait to make the investments that matter most to you?

Don't wait.

Create a living plan,
not just a dying plan.

Traditionally, estate planning focuses on preparation for an inevitable day that none of us look forward to and all of us wish would never come. Because we don't like to think about it, we tend to push away estate planning. Yet we know we need to get the estate in proper order.

To make estate planning more meaningful, think of it as what you can do **today** for yourself, your heirs, and for others. You'll be able to witness and participate in the joy others receive because of your choices. Consequently, you receive even greater joy as you observe the results of the generosity you bestow on others.

To help you understand this shift in thinking, consider these common-yet-necessary planning questions:

1. How much do you want each of your heirs to receive from your estate?
2. At what age do you want them to receive the funds?
3. Do you want them to receive the funds outright or in trust?
4. Do you want to give money or assets to charity? If you do, how much do you want to give?
5. Would you like to pay the least amount of estate taxes?
6. How would you like to pay your estate taxes?

These are the commonly asked, estate-planning issues. Some are more significant than others, which I'll explain in later chapters.

15

If you don't answer them,
Uncle Sam will answer them for you.

By not deciding on these things, you have decided to let someone else make decisions for you.

Let's say you've answered the above questions. Now that you have, you assume everything is in order.

Have you wrapped up everything that's important? Are you finished with every concern now that the documents are drafted and signed?

Maybe.

Could something be missing because you haven't had the opportunity to bring your heart to bear on your planning? Have you had the chance to invest your deepest passion in the planning process?

How would you feel to know you've exhausted all the available planning options?

Even more important:

- Have you made your deepest desires and dreams known to those who will receive an inheritance from you?
- Do they know what motivates you to make decisions about your wealth?
- Are you and your family aware of the impact your wealth has now and will have after you're gone?

Rethink and revise the common estate-planning questions; this time, connect your heart before you respond. As you answer these six questions, can you see how they lead you to a deeper understanding of planning for you, your family, and your estate?

1. In what ways do you want to inspire your heirs with the inheritance you plan to leave them?
2. After you consider the level of their maturity, what impact will the planned inheritance have on them?
3. What will "equal and fair" look like in light of the degree to which you trust each heir? Do you trust each heir to the same degree?
4. Do you believe your generosity could have a profound impact of greater good on others and society around you? Who and what organizations have had an impact on you?
5. Did you know paying estate taxes are optional?
6. What creative planning options would you like to use to remove estate taxes and accomplish your planning goals and objectives?

Questions like these can direct you to a more meaningful wealth-planning experience and unlock what's inside your heart and the possible impact of your wealth.

Does your estate planning create energy and excitement about what you can do with your wealth? Do you know with confidence that your plan will prevent what our family as well as other families have experienced?

Do you want a clear plan that allows you to live your dreams?

To have a wealth with no regrets life and future is like building the beautiful million dollar home that when you move in it feels and functions just like you envisioned it would.

Planning with a no regrets mindset and following a thorough process that helps you get beyond the financial decisions that need to be made allows you do to this.

Why not excite your heart, emotions, mind, relationships, and generosity?

What Now?

1. Do you believe your deepest feelings about what matters most to you such as your lifestyle needs, what you desire as an inheritance for your heirs as well as your charitable concerns and desires have been heard and understood by your advisors?

2. Would any part of your estate plan change if you considered a *made-just-for-you living plan* instead of a set of documents that prepares your assets to transfer when you die?

3. While you're alive, wouldn't it be fun to see the fruit of your hard work and the positive impact it has on others?

4. What is the one thing holding you back from doing more with your wealth right now that if you did it would create excitement energy for you?

Wealth With No Regrets is a focus on the desires of your heart in motion now.

My success, part of it certainly,
is that I have focused in on a few things.
—Bill Gates

3. Straight from the Heart

What is most important to you?

I encourage you to listen to your heart or what a friend calls "the better part of himself." If you do, you'll not only act wisely, but you'll respond from that deeper source. You'll join passion and excitement with clear thinking and thorough planning.

Wealth is far more than the figures on your net-worth balance sheet. It starts with the heart and involves your life, your relationships, and your resources.

Just as a well-run business is driven by a carefully thought-out and executed strategy, so is sound wealth planning.

Having clarity about what you truly want opens the door to possibilities you may not have realized were available. Good planning engages all aspects of wealth into an arrangement that:

- gives you pleasure today;
- protects for tomorrow;
- makes you enthusiastic for life;
- keeps you focused on living out your purpose.

Ultimately, your planning should give you hope, confidence, and peace of mind that your objectives are being achieved.

What is most important to you?

Do you want to spend the time and energy to make more money?
If the answer is yes, then for what purpose?

Your limited resource is time, and your abundant resource is money. The question then becomes: What amount of money would you give to do more of what matters most to you?

Here are three significant words to engage your heart:

Believe.

Listen.

Expect.

Believe

Believe you are more than the things you possess.
Believe you have something to give back to others, even beyond money.
Believe you can do more with the resources you have.
Believe you can achieve the desires of your heart.

Listen

Listen to the quiet voice of your heart.
Listen to your spouse.
Listen to your heirs and hear what matters to them.
Listen to the voices of the people in need around you.

Expect

Expect the impossible to become possible.
Expect to be heard and understood.
Expect more from your planning, and to understand it.
Expect more from your trusted advisors so you can achieve your goals.
Expect deeper, more engaging conversation about what you want to do.
Most of all, expect more from yourself.

You've worked hard, been lucky or blessed, and you're affluent. You still have many opportunities available to you.

There are outstanding opportunities available to affluent people—for special individuals like you—because you can make choices that many individuals can't.

Yet many prosperous people don't take advantage of the strategic planning opportunities available to them in the area of tax breaks and efficient passing of inheritances and gifts to charity. *They squander away their resources because they don't know the options available or they don't know how to decide on the right options for their situation.*

When there is a lack of clarity about what you want to do with your wealth it leads to a milieu of options that your advisors present to you. But more options and a lack of clarity about what you want will likely result in confusion, indecision, and inaction.

You *will* leave a legacy.

BUT

only you can determine the kind of legacy.

You have a purpose in life. Because you're still alive you haven't totally fulfilled that purpose.

Think what that statement means.

- You can do immeasurable good in the world.
- You have the ability and the resources to help many and it requires little effort.
- You can inspire your heirs.

Don't avoid a discussion about what matters to you because you don't think it's relevant to the planning discussion.

If the cost of the ensuing dialogue about your heart and what matters to you hinders you from talking about it, I suggest to you another way—and I'm convinced it is a better way.

The other way begins with a depth of understanding about you—what matters to you, and what you really want to do. This is done best in a discovery session with someone trained to ask the right questions to help you draw out the answers.

This can result in a set of clear and measurable objectives that resonate with your heart's desires.

How often have you left a meeting with one of your financial advisors and thought, *That was amazing?*

Did you smile and say, "That was an enjoyable experience?"

If you're typical, you'll admit that hasn't been your experience.

That is how you could feel after a discovery session with your most trusted advisor. That happens when you're allowed to open your heart and discuss your deepest emotions about your wealth, concerns, and desires.

Check the items your current plan accomplishes for you.

Do you have an estate plan that:

- ☐ eliminates gift and estate taxes?
- ☐ provides for an appropriate and well thought-out inheritance?
- ☐ frees you to live out the desires you have for your wealth *right now?*
- ☐ allows you to use your charitable giving to enlarge your heirs' inheritances?
- ☐ answers your questions about transitioning your business to the next generation?
- ☐ implements the strategies to leverage your assets for the greatest personal benefit?
- ☐ gives you or your spouse absolute confidence in your estate plan?
- ☐ accomplishes all your objectives?
- ☐ enables you to be anxiety-free about what happens to your assets?
- ☐ eliminates the concerns your planned inheritance will create for your heirs?
- ☐ provides for the alignment of all your resources to a clearly understood purpose?

If you checked off less than **seven** of these boxes you still have a lot of planning to do!

If you have all the planning answers you're looking for, stop reading.

But if you want

- **confidence** you're living with your wealth as you desire, and you'll achieve your goals for your family and charity, and you'll pay no estate taxes, starting today.
- **hope** for where you're going, and the impact your wealth will have on your family and others.
- **peace of mind** that you have seized every opportunity and triumphed over every challenge.

You can't afford

to stop reading.

Looking back, I recall conversations with my dad when he made comments such as:

- "Mom should be fine."
- "I've put everything in place so there shouldn't be a problem."
- "I trust you guys will be able to work things out harmoniously."

My father was mistaken.

Several times I asked my mom about the estate-planning process. She trusted my dad when he told her he was getting everything in order. She had no reason not to trust him, but in this case it's not a matter of trust, it's a matter of being involved, knowing, and doing.

What now?

Get used to that question because it's the most pressing one I'll ask. It's really to ask about your planning.

1. Your answer will lead to additional questions about available opportunities.
2. What do I do *now* to make my life significant and remain significant?
3. What do I do *now* about the wealth I've accumulated?

What you do in your planning has implications beyond what you do for yourself. It will extend to your family for generations and can—if done right—profoundly impact and assist others who need help.

Consider this:
If you decide correctly,
your legacy will inspire and
bless the generations that follow.

When your planning captures in written form exactly what *you* want, you'll be able to live with confidence, have hope for the lasting legacy you want to create, peace of mind for yourself, and your family, and in how you'll bless others.

What Now?

1. Have you been asked enough questions about your life, what matters to you, and what you really want to do with the wealth you have?
2. Are you confident that every idea important to you has been uncovered and discussed?
3. Does your plan represent the path to your big desired future that you envision for yourself, your family and the causes that matter to you deeply?
4. Did the discovery phase of planning with your advisor make you feel you exhausted all applicable aspects of your life and wealth and what you want to do with it?

Wealth With No Regrets is about more than assets on your personal balance sheet.

The happiest moments of my life
have been the few which I have passed at home
in the bosom of my family.
—Thomas Jefferson

4. Lucky or Blessed?

"I'm just lucky I guess . . ." is how one affluent person responded when asked why he had been so successful.

Or perhaps not.

Here is a true story. A man in his seventies immigrated to this country to run innovative businesses. He was involved in cutting-edge products that eventually became household brands. He was admired and envied for his technical expertise and business savvy.

He never became rich.

He didn't receive stock options before the companies he operated were purchased or went public. He was always on the front end of the innovation, but he moved on to the front end of another innovative venture before the big payoff. Even though almost every venture made a lot of money, it never worked out for him to participate in the bounty.

He wasn't less smart than those who received the big payout; in fact, he was probably smarter. His business acumen wasn't less significant in the results the companies experienced, but his *timing* in the business cycle wasn't as fortunate for him as it was for others.

Regardless of who *you* are, or how talented you may be—and if you're honest with yourself—you have to wonder:

- Why have I done so much better than others I know?
- Why me?
- My neighbor or classmate is as intelligent as I am, but that person didn't make it and I did. Why?

That's the beginning: You face the reality that you're successful, *but how did you become so successful while many around you didn't?*

Did you become affluent because you were superior to others? Probably you can say, "I have an ability—a gift—to make money."

Or perhaps you say something like, "I started at exactly the right time and had favorable conditions along with the help and encouragement of a number of people."

What is the reason for your success?

If you consider yourself blessed, then planning is something that goes beyond what you can preserve for yourself.

When you understand your life as being bigger than your accomplishments, the typical estate-planning questions fall short.

Consider the typical questions:

1. How much money do I want to give my heirs?
2. How much of my estate do I want to keep from the government?
3. How much—if anything—do I want to give to charity?

They're good questions, but they're inadequate.

They don't include enough of the right questions.

Being blessed points to receiving gifts beyond your abilities. Therefore the responsibility in planning is far greater than making a decision about a percentage of assets of heirs and the timing of such distribution.

Wealth is more than money. It's more than profits, percentages, and timed distributions.

Wealth is more than the assets that show up on your net-worth balance sheet. Isn't wealth more than what you have and can continue to accumulate for yourself?

Because wealth is more, planning should be about more too.

What Now?

1. What's the reason for your success? Was it simply "the luck of the draw" or was it more?
2. You've been blessed to have so much, so what can you do to add to the blessing?
3. If you could do only one more thing with your wealth in your lifetime and it would double your happiness, what would it be?

Wealth With No Regrets is living responsibly with the use of all resources.

From everyone who has been given much,
much will be required in return;
and when someone has been entrusted with much,
even more will be required.
—Jesus

5. What Do I Still Need to Do?

Estate planning is a massive undertaking, isn't it? It seems easier to leave it for someone else to deal with after you're gone. In fact, you're extremely busy and have an abundance of resources that allow you to be financially secure for your remaining years.

But do you need to do something more?

One of the great kings in Jewish history, King Hezekiah, was given a message from God through the leading prophet of the day. "Set your affairs in order, for you are going to die. You will not recover from this illness."[3]

The king didn't do the responsible thing. Instead he engrossed himself in self-gratifying activities. Ironically, his behavior led to the destruction of his wealth, and his family became servants for the Babylonian empire. When confronted because of his behavior he became indifferent. He didn't seem concerned about his legacy. "For the king was thinking, 'At least there will be peace and security during my lifetime.' "[4]

---

[3] 2 Kings 20:1.
[4] 2 Kings 20:19b.

Through his indifference, the king concluded he was fine now and things would go well during his remaining years. It was as if he said, "It won't be until after I'm gone, that dreadful things happen. My heirs can deal with sorting out the details of my wealth."

By contrast, my father wanted to leave a strong legacy to us and others. If we had discussed King Hezekiah and his life, he probably would have said, "This will never happen to me and my family."

But it did.

My father wasn't apathetic; however, no one showed him how to finish strong and preserve his legacy. Despite the planning expertise of his advisors, my father didn't know there was a better way to leave things.

How do you know you won't make the same mistake my entrepreneurial father did? As I mentioned earlier in this book, seven out of ten successful, wise, and affluent people make the same mistake.

Wealthy families that plan responsibly understand the impact of their decisions. They decide to make an intentional positive impact now that lasts for generations.

By planning the no regrets way you're setting the boundaries—the guidelines—not only for the immediate generation but for several generations.

Don't focus on what others insist you should or ought to do. This is your wealth. You have the right as well as the responsibility to make those decisions.

The choices you make, right now, about your wealth will have a far-reaching impact.

As an affluent person, you're different from most people around you. Not better, not worse, just different. Decisions about how to distribute your possessions are only part of the issue. You face more serious decisions.

What do *you feel responsible to* achieve with the wealth you've accumulated?

Bob Buford, author of *Half Time* and a successful man in business, said he tries to get people not to focus on what they've done but to ask, "What do I do with my life now that I have all this stuff?"

Here's another way of asking the same question: How does my life become significant and how does it remain significant after I'm gone?

Significance is about capturing who you are and giving back of yourself and resources for the greater good of others.

Your legacy can take on significant meaning and last for generations. The way you live now and distribute wealth can bring honor within your family and to others for generations.

What Now?

1. How do you know that your estate plan won't create confusion and misrepresent you and your most desired legacy?
2. What really matters to you about your wealth and what you pass on to others?
3. Have you written down your concerns and discussed them with someone who understands planning as well as matters of wealth beyond the money – priorities, values, family, relationships, generosity, and making an impact?

Wealth With No Regrets is a living opportunity.

The optimist sees the opportunity
in every difficulty.
—Winston Churchill

6. The Deeper Question

Susan T. Buffett, the late wife of billionaire Warren Buffett, was in line to inherit her husband's fortune had she not died before her husband.

"Susie and I always assumed that she would inherit my Berkshire stock and be the one who oversaw the distribution of our wealth to society, where both of us had always said it would go.

"And Susie would have enjoyed overseeing the process. She was a little afraid of it, in terms of scaling up. But she would have liked doing it, and would have been very good at it. And she would have really stepped on the gas."[5]

"Susie was two years younger than I," Mr. Buffett wrote, "and women usually live longer than men." The assumption was she would inherit the fortune and give it away.

One expectation you can have about life expectancy, is that you ultimately really never know when anyone will die.

---

[5] *Fortune* magazine interview with Warren Buffett, June 25, 2006. http://money.cnn.com2006/06/25/magazines/fortune/charity2.fortune/index. htm.

Now is the time. Because:
- you don't know when your last day will be;
- your heirs need to know your intentions;
- you need to see the reactions of your heirs about your intentions;
- you can eliminate estate taxes;
- heirs tend to need an inheritance sooner than later.

Consider the story of a woman named Esther from Jewish history. She became queen at a time when the Persians controlled most of the then-known world. The king chooses her as his queen because of her beauty, and in rising to the throne, she doesn't reveal her Jewish ancestry.

Later she learns a wicked man named Haman has given a large sum of money to the Persian treasury. In doing so, he bribes the king to enact a law that gives citizens the right to kill all Jews.

Esther's uncle, Mordecai, comes to see the queen and makes her aware of the situation. He tells her that she is the only one who can save her people.

Here's what he says: "Don't think for a moment that because you're in the palace you will escape when all other Jews are killed. If you keep quiet at a time like this, deliverance and relief for the Jews will arise from some other place, but you and your relatives will die. *Who knows if perhaps you were made queen for just such a time as this?"* [Italics mine.][6]

---

[6] The Book of Esther, 4:13-14.

That was Mordecai's challenge and it has resonated through the ages. "Who knows if perhaps you were made queen for just such a time as this?"

You have accumulated means beyond what you need for survival. You are in a place of influence both within your own family and outside of it.

Why now?

- There are people to be helped.
- There are problems in society to be solved.
- There is opportunity to get relationships set right.

Do you sense there are opportunities for you to seize or problems to solve with your wealth? If you don't do those things, will you feel you've missed your calling or purpose in life?

The concept of ownership changes when your focus is to have no regrets. You're in possession of a great deal of resources and you're responsible for them when you're here on earth. You can't take those things with you; therefore, they're yours to manage while you are here.

It wasn't until I grasped the idea of being a manager that I realized keeping assets is only for a time. "Why not use them for the good of others," I asked myself, "and give away what you can't keep?"

This was an important insight for me. Growing up, I knew my father was quite generous. Quietly and sometimes anonymously, he gave away 35 percent of his income. I thought the remaining 65 percent was ours to keep.

The missionary martyr James Elliot said, "He is no fool who gives what he cannot keep, to gain that which he cannot lose."[7]

You become the benefactor of all that you give away and cannot keep anyway. That's a legacy.

Before you leave this world, you have the opportunity *as well as the responsibility* to make thoughtful and thorough decisions about where, how, and the purpose of the impact of your wealth.

Do you believe you have an obligation to do something with your wealth that's bigger than you are?

That's the deeper question.

Noblesse Oblige

This French phrase (noh-bles-oh-bleezh) has become part of the English language and incorporates the idea that privilege entails responsibility. Being a person of noble birth (and that implied wealth) assumed this individual had the responsibility to lead others.

In American English, the term carries a broader meaning: Those who are capable of helping the less fortunate have a duty to do so (and that usually means with money).

---

[7] Jim Elliot, missionary martyr.

What Now?

1. Do you have a sense of obligation to use your resources for something much bigger than you are?
2. Because you can't take it with you, what do you need to do to ensure that the resources left behind will be properly managed?
3. What do you need to do to put your resources to work *right now* to begin fulfilling the greater responsibility to which you feel called?
4. What is the one question you have, that if you had an answer, would unleash a flood of generosity for greater impact and more enjoyment for you?

Wealth With No Regrets is a significant life purpose in action.

Most people spend more time and energy
going around problems than in trying
to solve them.
—Henry Ford

7. What's *My* Purpose?

Jim continues to run a highly profitable business he started 40 years ago. The business is also his passion. However, he remains at a point of indecision about what to do with it. Should he sell or keep it? He also continues to procrastinate on getting his estate in order.

What happens if he continues as he is without doing anything? Who will buy the business or who will sell it for what he thinks it is worth?

These two questions bring to the forefront of his mind that he doesn't have a successor within the family to take over his life's work. What does he do about that?

Beyond the logistics of selling the business or selecting a successor, he can't visualize what his days would look like without doing the same thing he is now. He continues to work 60 hours a week and has no hobbies, so without the business, what would he do with his time?

If he had a vision for his life, a purpose for it, decisions would come much easier and he'd know what to do today with his business and his wealth.

He's stuck doing the same things he's been doing his entire career that was founded on achieving success. But now that he's achieved more than he ever expected, he asks, "What now?"

Think about yourself. When you started out in your twenties you knew where you wanted to go. And you weren't going to quit until you had achieved the success you desired. You had a plan and you lived that plan successfully.

You still need a plan—but now it's a different kind. You need a plan for your life and wealth.

Who would have thought the final two decades of your life could be the most exciting? They can be exactly that if you shore up your purpose and align your wealth with it.

Not knowing your life purpose isn't the same as not having a purpose.

Everyone has a unique purpose. Discovering and living your purpose and understanding the purpose for your wealth is an important secret to having no regrets.

I believe my father didn't settle on a life purpose that would give meaning and success to his final years on earth. He decided he had made enough money and didn't need more. He was no longer interested in building the business bigger.

He needed a significant purpose instead of a success purpose.

Knowing your purpose in being alive right now—at this time in history—needs to be a significant factor in your planning. You're not wealthy apart from being who you are, who you were created to be.

You're not your assets. Your wealth is an important part of life, but it's not everything. You're a person beyond what you do or how you earn money.

I've frequently reminded my mother that Dad was more than the business he built and the organization he ran. Whether the business stays or goes was insignificant compared to the man, Dale Spencer.

I've learned that a successful business reaches a point of satisfaction—where entrepreneurs and executives can say, "I've met and exceeded my dreams."

Yet they keep on.

Why do they do that?

I'd like to explain their reasoning. Sammy is a very successful man with great affluence who could have sold his business. Instead, he sought his life purpose while going about his wealth planning. He discovered his purpose was fulfilled by keeping the business so he could give more money away. That is, the business served his philanthropic life purpose.

He needed to run it in a different way, with the employment of someone he could train to fulfill his objectives. That left him free to mentor people and give the profits away.

There must be a burning reason to keep going forward and enjoying what you're doing. If you're not still enjoying it, your blessing has probably become a burden.

Great coaches ask, "Do you own your business or does your business own you?" That's a great question whether you're an entrepreneur or executive. It's another way to ask, "Are you and your business the same thing?"

Freedom comes as a result of owning the business in a way that keeps you excited about going to work each day. Or your freedom might come from selling the business. Maybe you need to change how you operate your organization. Maybe it's time to wave good-bye.

Regardless, don't do anything new or different until you understand your purpose.

Why have you achieved so much?

What makes you special?

You are special because you have achieved what many have only dreamed about.

But you might be thinking, There is no way to walk away from the work I've spent my life building. It is the only thing I know.

I totally agree, but that prompts me to ask: How do you get a dog to let go of a dry bone? The answer is you give the dog a bone with meat on it.

"Purpose" is the bone with meat on it. Why would a dog continue chewing on a dry bone if you offer real food?

You need to chew on a bone with meat on it. That's what you've done for years, but maybe you need a new bone. If you discover your purpose, it may result in keeping the business, but doing it differently, or you may feel your purpose is to leave the business entirely.

**What you do isn't as important
as acting from a compelling sense of purpose.**

When you merge your talent and your passion with a purpose, it can bring magic into your life.

54

What Now?

1. Have you discovered your life's purpose?
2. What are some things that fire you up and make it exciting to get out of bed in the morning?
3. Why haven't you pursued your life purpose?
4. Because you have the means to do most anything you want, what's holding you back?

Part 2:

Advantages of Planning the Wealth With No Regrets Way

Getting different results requires
a different approach to
wealth planning.

Wealth With No Regrets planning is an investment in your family and your legacy.

Don't begin until you count the cost.
—Jesus

8. Count the Costs

As I've pointed out, a 20-year study indicates that seven out of ten estates fail to transfer wealth successfully to the next generation. Now here is the rest of the story on failure.[8] If you continue to track the "successful" 30 percent, 70 percent of these fail to pass wealth to the next generation. This results in a total of **90 percent of estates vanishing by the third generation.**[9]

If you fail as this study indicates, your wealth will not endure past your grandchildren's generation. A proverb claims, "Good people leave an inheritance to their grandchildren."[10]

Here's an example of what I mean. Joe Robbie was the owner of the Miami Dolphins and the stadium in which they played. After his death, the family was forced to sell assets, including the team and the stadium he built, to pay the estate tax, which was due within nine months of his passing.

---

[8] Failure is defined in the study as involuntary loss of control of assets.

[9] Out of 100 families, 70 fail to provide ongoing wealth for their heirs, which results in 30 successful families. Of those 30 families, 70 percent will fail, which results in about nine successful families out of 100 by the third generation.

[10] Book of Proverbs, 13:22.

Robbie's family publicly incurred hardship and conflict to the point that one heir reportedly said, "My dad's planning was so bad that it caused friction between my sister and me."

"As much as Mr. Robbie produced for his children, I'm sure he's turning in his grave," Dade County Circuit Court Judge Ronald Friedman said to the family. "I'm sure this is the last thing Mr. Robbie wanted to see."[11]

This story illustrates the two types of costs to failure of proper planning.

First, there is up to 55 percent estate tax on the value of all your assets above the estate-tax deduction.[12] In addition, there are planning fees that cost one to three percent of the gross estate to settle the estate appropriately upon the death.

The second cost is exponentially devastating: the breakdown of your family and a diminished legacy. This could mean no longer gathering together at the holidays, and cutting off communication with one another.

The legacy and good name of the patriarch and matriarch are tainted. The research study evaluated the causes of failure and found it was attributable to inadequate preparation in relational wealth planning.

As I pointed out earlier, only three percent of the next generation's estate-transfer failure is due to improperly prepared estate documents. Ninety-seven percent of the

---

[11] Media Matters for America, online article, "Limbaugh misleads on Joe Robbie and the Dolphins to bash estate tax." December 10, 2010.
[12] The current law at the writing of this book states that the estate tax-deduction amount will be $1 million in 2013.

cause of failure is due to broken trust, closed lines of communication, and lack of a clear wealth vision.

Like a shrewd businessman, my father wanted as much bang for every dollar spent as he could get. The scale of his dealings changed, but his desire for a good deal never did.

For instance, my father was a car enthusiast buying and trading vehicles frequently. He started with Cadillacs and Lincolns. By the time I was in my teens, he had graduated to Mercedes-Benz. In later years he did the same with the Bentley and Rolls Royce. Despite his ability to pay full price, the excitement was getting a deal.

When it came to estate planning, he looked at it through the same lens—getting a good deal, when he should have been looking for value. By the end of working with his planners, he knew he hadn't gotten a good bargain, but also didn't know how little value he had received.

After the 88-page plan was finally complete and signed, the last invoice from the attorney came in the mail. I happened to be with him when he opened it.

I witnessed the anger in his eyes as he said, "What did I get for this? What a rip off." He felt the price was outrageous for the value he gained. But little did he know the depths of that reality.

My father would be embarrassed and deeply disappointed by the result his failed estate planning had on his accumulated wealth, family, and legacy. In spite of his best intentions, efforts, good advisors, and an 88-page estate document, his plan failed to accomplish what he ultimately wanted.

In trying to straighten out everything, our family paid three times what he originally spent on his estate plan. We paid it to satisfy conflicts that could have been resolved if my father had received wise counsel from a specialist. It cost the family and his legacy far more than dollars could calculate.

I can tell you that my father would have paid three times what he did if he knew he would have ended up in the category of families who were among the 30 percent. *He didn't know he had that choice.*

**You pay the price of having an incomplete
plan that doesn't capture your deeper intent.
You enjoy the benefits of receiving value
of a plan that captures your desired future.**

Failure is more likely when affluent families follow the traditional estate-planning process just like my father did. They're not the results that successful people like my dad want or deserve.

Too much planning is done from a focus on tax advantages and not enough on life and family planning.

A cost that adds valuable solutions to resolve problems or allows you to pursue something that matters to you is an investment. Here's the real question: What is the best investment of your resources to accomplish what you want done?

In many cases you can pay between one and three percent of your gross estate to plan and settle your estate. If you delay or do nothing you or your family will pay this much or more. However, if your approach to planning is more than a business decision then planning becomes an investment in your life, your family, your legacy, and causes that matter to you deeply.

The United States government says that when you die, someone must complete IRS form 706. In that document you *must* list every asset—your entire estate.

If you complete the form 706 now, you're making an investment while you still have control. If you don't do it, others are required to do it later and they probably won't know the details of your life and estate.

When we filled out the IRS form 706 after Dad died, we didn't know details about many of the assets. For example, my parents' Florida vacation home was owned in my father's name individually, and therefore it had to go through probate. That is only one, small example of the additional costs as well as lengthy aggravation that transpired.

If you delay or do nothing, you can pay the IRS up to 55 percent of the value of your estate. Or invest in the right planning now and more fully enjoy wealth today.

But there's more.

After spending a lot of time talking with my mother, both of us realized my father's desires for contributions hadn't taken place. My parents' charitable desires had been greatly overlooked from an estate-tax planning perspective.

For instance, Dad mentioned a family foundation in his estate document, but it was never funded with any assets. The estate-planning attorney didn't realize how important generous giving was to my parents. Therefore, he didn't understand the details of the assets enough to position them so my mother would have ensured her lifestyle with a stream of income without worry, provided an appropriate inheritance, and also funded the foundation. That would have allowed my mom to spend the rest of her life giving away millions of dollars to the charities that mattered so much to them.

You have the opportunity now to make an investment out of your hard work, remove the possibility of a 55 percent loss, and invest in your family and your legacy, if you plan right today. Turn your planning into an opportunity to achieve your objectives while you can experience the joy. Build trust and open communication with your family so they'll learn what matters most to you.

---

70 Percent of Estate Transitions Fail

Failure rates are consistent regardless of the country, tax laws, or the timing within the economic cycle.

Causes of failure:

60 percent = Breakdown of communication and trust within the family unit.

25 percent = Inadequately prepared heirs.

15 percent = Tax, legal, and accounting issues.

Only 3 percent of failures are a result of the professional field's inability to properly execute their trade of drafting and properly written estate documents.[13]

---

[13] Op. cit. *Preparing Heirs.*

Those whom you love and trust deserve to know your wishes and the expressions of your heart while you're still alive.

You can't put a price on getting wealth planning done right. When properly done, it isn't really a cost but an investment, with compounding return, in the life of your spouse, your family, your legacy, and society.

Even without major conflicts, the lack of clear desire, along with trust and communication about the plan, leads to the slowing of estate settlement that unnecessarily increases the legal costs. If you add family conflict to the situation, it brings about the misuse of estate assets on frivolous expenditures as members' family act out of pain and disappointment, and also increases the legal costs to settle disputes.

The wisest and most recognized teacher in history said it this way:

But don't begin until you count the cost. For who would begin construction of a building without first calculating the cost to see if there is enough money to finish it? Otherwise, you might complete only the foundation before running out of money, and then everyone would laugh at you. They would say, "There's the person who started that building and couldn't afford to finish it.[14]

You pay the price of having an incomplete plan that doesn't capture your deeper intent. You enjoy the benefits of receiving the value of a plan that captures your desired intent right now and future.

---

[14] Jesus, Book of Luke, 14:28-30.

What Now?

1. What might it cost you today and in the future—financially and relationally—if you don't do more planning than you've done so far?
2. What would it be worth to you to invest in your planning and family preparations *today*?
3. Which option appeals to you? Do you invest today so you can experience the joy of seeing problems solved and opportunities seized? Or do you want your family to spend many times more money after you're gone?
4. If it were a matter of investing $50 or $100 today to protect $1000 for tomorrow, wouldn't you do that? And if that investment meant ensuring your legacy and family's future wouldn't that be of value beyond the money – even priceless?

Wealth With No Regrets planning is knowing where you want to go and having a map to get there.

It's hard to be aggressive when you're confused.
—Vince Lombardi

9. Five Advantages of No Regrets Wealth Planning

If you count the cost and decide you want to increase your probability of success, you'll be among the three of ten families who transition their estates well.

Here is what good wealth planning should accomplish:

1. You live now with confidence and peace about finishing strong.
2. You intentionally inspire your heirs to know who they are and to live out their purpose.
3. You control wealth and decide where it goes now and later.
4. You experience a sense of purposeful giving.
5. You implement a creative and actionable plan.
6. Isn't this what you and your spouse want from your planning?

The no regrets wealth approach demands more investment in the front end of planning; however, the end result makes the effort worth it.

You can easily fool yourself into thinking you've covered everything once you've written a will and created trusts to protect your assets. If you've done that much, you've *started* with the essential documentation.

But that's only the beginning.

69

Estate planning that accomplishes these goals is ultimately about living with your wealth now, while you're alive. You can have a say in what happens with your assets in the present and when you're gone, with the right planning.

Unless you are already experiencing the five advantages of no regrets wealth planning, you deserve more. The chances are, you haven't exhausted the possibilities available to you.

- You can give more.
- You can pay no estate taxes.
- You can leave an appropriate inheritance now— when they need it.
- You can live now and do the things that matter most to you.
- You can rest with peace knowing you've done *all* you can with your wealth.
- You can plan from your heart and enjoy the fruit of your labor today.

Spencer/Murphey

Wealth With No Regrets
planning gives confidence and peace of mind to everyone.

We are more easily persuaded, in general,
by the reasons we ourselves discover
than by those which are given to us by others.
—Blaise Pascal

10. Live Now with Confidence and Peace

I'm not a big pro football fan, but I enjoy watching the New England Patriots. When they march onto the field, they step out with confidence. They expect to win; they're not prepared to lose.

They've already put in the time, the work, and the training. They've mapped out, practiced, and understood the game plan.

What's the result?

- They're clear on what they want to accomplish.
- They have a plan to win the game.
- They know their individual responsibilities.
- They are united—members of a team—and each player knows what he can expect from the other teammates.
- They play the game with the assurance that they'll win.

The coach's role is to devise a plan the players understand and execute. Then he inspires, empowers, and encourages the implementation of the plan.

All wealthy individuals should have an advisor serving them in a similar way. Your planning should result in an experience of restful assurance and confidence. That means you've covered every available possibility, and you've kept your plan updated as your circumstances evolved.

Confidence that you have a plan from your heart makes your desires clear and allows you to build trust through open communication with your advisors and family. If you don't do the right planning, in the right way, you could lose the game.

You can live in restful assurance and confidence. Isn't that what you really want?

But achieving that reality is more than drafting properly written estate documents. Confidence is deepened when you have an easy to understand plan that captures what matters to you beyond the money.

My dad didn't speak about what he had set up. He didn't because he couldn't articulate what the attorney, using legal language, drafted. It wasn't written in plain, easy to understand terms. My father was an intelligent man, but what the expert wrote might as well have been a foreign language. In fact, it was a foreign language.

As I wrote those words, I thought of my wife, Lori, who spent several months in China after graduating from college. One of the first challenges she faced after stepping off the plane was communicating to the taxi driver where she wanted to go.

A briefing prior to the trip educated her that Chinese taxi drivers will nod yes even when they're unclear about where to take you. She was prepared by having her destination written in Chinese on a business card by a local translator. He kept the language clear and simple enough for the taxi driver to understand.

Using that method repeatedly, Lori navigated through China with confidence and peace of mind. Even more, along the way she began to understand and speak the language.

By contrast, the legal jargon of my father's documents created a language barrier. When a plan is written in plain language, it increases confidence and the desire to communicate the plan and its intention with others. It also increases the understanding about the impact the plan will have on you and others.

Did you create your wealth by running a business according to a set of legal documents or a list of rules?

Of course not. Your keen mind for a clear strategy and the execution was essential. As the saying goes, "you did it your way." And your way led to success in business.

- How much time, sweat, and thought went into creating your successful business?
- Was your effort focused primarily on constructing legal documents?
- Or did you focus on the creation of what you wanted to accomplish?
- Did you set up your business to go into effect at some future date after you're gone, or right now, while you're around to see it become a reality and to have some control over what happens afterward?

Don't wait until you're in poor health to get serious about planning.

My father was 40 years old when he had his first heart attack. After multiple heart procedures, he was told at age 52, he needed a heart transplant. The poor health reports continued even after receiving his new heart.

The planning process was almost unbearable at that point while trying to manage his health. Having to daily face his own mortality and plan at the same time compounded stress.

Waiting for these moments to get serious about planning exposes a mindset that estate planning is primarily about death preparation.

The sooner you do no regrets wealth planning, the more options are available to you. If you plan for the future with the care, commitment, and inner desire that you infused into building toward success, the payoff is enormous in savings and growth.

Having Wealth With No Regrets is as much about having a present life plan as it is a what happens at death plan.

How do you live with confidence and peace?

1. The two CEOs in an affluent family need to be in agreement about your wealth, incorporating both perspectives into the planning.

And there are two CEOs in an affluent family.

Typically, the one who made the money is CEO—the chief executive officer, and the other is the chief *emotional* officer. Both need to be comfortable in their roles and confide in each other. Too often the chief emotional officer isn't part of the planning process.

My father failed by not involving my mom in the planning process. In his defense, however, a law office is a tough place to get motivated to talk about big decisions that are particularly close to the heart.

The chief executive officer understands the assets and financial make-up of the wealth; the chief emotional officer is in touch with the relational influences of wealth on the family. They need each other for their different perspectives.

Both CEOs have ideas about the philanthropic nature of what to do with your wealth. Confidence begins to surface when both have the opportunity to express their perspectives to influence wealth planning.

2. You become confident and peaceful with open communication with the family about your wealth.
When done correctly and with the help of an independent third party, conversation about the family wealth becomes productive in building family unity.

77

In the absence of communication about wealth, family members are left to speculate from their own grid of experience and personal biases. That leads to divisive thinking and nonproductive action. Properly done, family meetings allow any issues—often unforeseen—to surface while there is time to resolve them, or at least speak to the issues in a productive way.

3. Making the complex simple. If you're affluent, you have wealth that is millions of dollars beyond simple. The assets that make up your wealth are no longer uncomplicated and neither are the solutions. Confidence comes when you learn to simplify the complex.

You should be able to articulate or explain a well-established, no regrets wealth plan on a single page of paper. Breaking down the assets and their structures into their simplest parts so both CEOs can understand is essential for building confidence and restful assurance.

Think about your business. Can you articulate your business strategy on one page so that others can understand what you do?

4. A good wealth plan is one the family easily understands. It can be understood by trustees and all advisors to the family.

One of the major barriers is a plan filled with technical jargon—the kind probably understood only by the estate-planning attorneys. But a confidence-producing wealth plan is one you can articulate in plain language and is based on the clear desires of your heart.

5. Confidence comes from planning beyond templates and boiler-plate documents. They need to show detailed and thorough planning so you can use your wealth for the greater good.

You and your situation are unique, so your plan should be customized to fit your situation. It should represent who you are, your life, and the legacy you desire to leave.

My first experience with estate planning occurred when I introduced my father and mother to a friend at a major investment-banking firm. Dad was in bad health and knew there was no detailed plan in place. I had no knowledge of the makeup or extent of our family's assets. We had never had a family meeting, so I had no idea about the extent of his wealth or what he wanted to happen with his assets. I knew my parents were wealthy, but little more than that.

Although we were unaware, the family needed a meeting to give us confidence that what my father owned would survive beyond him. We especially needed confidence that mom would be taken care of and a clear understanding of the roles we'd be asked to fulfill.

I took the risk in putting together a meeting, even though Dad could have misinterpreted my intentions.

Dad knew about the meeting weeks in advance, but he didn't say anything about the appointment until the night before the meeting. He tried to back out of the nine o'clock appointment.

"I don't want to go to that meeting," Dad said. "Let's call it off."

"We can't do that," I said. "It's after hours so no one will be there. I refuse to cancel on my friends at the last minute when there's no emergency."

Dad was obviously uncomfortable and made it clear he didn't want to keep the appointment.

"You have to go," I insisted. I responded to each objection and said, "I promise that you won't be required to make decisions or be forced to put any money with the investment manager."

When Dad realized I was determined to get him there, he stopped fighting me. I took both parents to the meeting. I was allowed to sit in while they spoke with the investment advisor, and I said nothing the whole time.

As soon as the investment adviser finished talking about what he does and the benefits of his company, he asked, "Any questions?"

My parents both shook their heads.

The advisor escorted us down the hall to the estate-planning attorney.

There he postulated about planning options typically utilized by people of my parent's financial means.

Looking back, I realize how badly that meeting really went. It didn't produce any confidence for my father or mother that something significant had taken place. In fact, neither of them understood most of the language the advisors used.

On the way to my house, Dad said, "I don't want to go back."

I agreed with his decision.

My mother didn't say much but she was confused and admitted, "I felt stupid."

"Part of the time they talked over my head," my father said, "and the rest of the time they talked down to me like I wasn't capable of comprehending opportunities or understanding how to live up to my challenges."

I had listened and I felt exactly the same way; I was as ignorant as my parents.

The appointment ended up being a conversation about transactional options, and the advisers talked mostly about planning tools and seemed intent to sell my parents on why they should use them. I thought, They make me feel as if a person is a round hole but their square peg should fit anyway.

Useful planning options were presented, but they weren't communicated properly. The result left my parents confused.

That should never have happened. The conversations didn't come close to highlighting opportunities for my parents' desire to be generous with the wealth they had accumulated.

Regardless of the language and the programs they offered, it's never effective until the desires of the heart of both CEOs are clear and the planning options address those concerns.

A discussion around possible transactions, without first understanding the desires of the heart, is useless for infusing confidence. They didn't know what my father wanted to do with his assets and made no serious attempt to reach his emotional level. Without getting to the heart, the conversation led to greater confusion and more anxiety about wealth and what to do with it.

Your wealth plan should produce confidence about how you achieve your dreams and plans for the use of your assets. You need a plan you can easily understand—one you're able to articulate for yourself, your family, and for anyone else.

The final sense of confidence comes from knowing that your plan has been implemented to your satisfaction. A guess or a wish that the strategies and techniques in your plan are executed isn't good enough to get rid of the nagging thought about whether you got certain things done. Do the funding of trusts and let someone make it happen for you.

It's your wealth.

Don't you deserve to feel ownership of the plan?

Does your current plan give you and your spouse the stand with confidence strength of conviction about your planning and the impact it is having and will have where it matters to you most?

What Now?

1. What level of understanding do you have about what your plan says and what it will do for you?
2. Are you and your spouse in complete agreement about your wealth plans?
3. What is one unresolved issue or concern about your wealth plans that you need to discuss with your spouse and your most trusted advisor?
4. What difference would it make in your life and marriage if you and your spouse were even a smidgen closer to an agreement about what is and will happen with your wealth today and in the future?

Wealth With No Regrets
planning intentionally inspires heirs to live their purpose.

If you raise children to feel that they can accomplish
any goal or task they decide on, you will have given
your children the greatest of all blessings.
—Brian Tracy

11. Intentionally Inspire Your Heirs

You don't have to do anything to inspire or motivate your heirs. If you plan well and listen to your deepest feelings, you'll inspire those who follow you.

They may be inspired to create their own story—a story that says who they are, what they want, and how they'll achieve their desired goals.

It's never too early—or too late—to inspire your heirs. One person who did it at exactly the right time was Dick Baidas.

Dick was the second-generation majority owner of one of the largest recreational vehicle retailers in the country. His youngest son, Loren, had graduated from college and worked on his own in the banking field.

In an informal conversation, Dick asked Loren if he had any interest in working at the family company. Loren initially said no. After time away from the family business and working for a different company, Loren had time to think about his direction. He then chose to make a commitment to himself and to his father to work at the company.

Loren was young, but he brought a confidence from being out on his own, and then was strategic about his entry into the business. His journey started at an early age, working after school and on weekends. He didn't come into the company with an entitlement mentality, but he willingly started at an entry-level position and worked his way to the top. Loren gradually earned the respect of his co-workers.

His father, Dick, lived a healthy lifestyle and was an avid runner when he was diagnosed with terminal pancreatic cancer. At only 58 years old, he was given just weeks to live.

At the time of the bad-health report, Loren had been running the business with his dad for eight years.

As a result, it was a seamless and natural transition for Loren to step into his dad's role, even though it came earlier than either had planned. There was no mass exodus of employees.

That's not all. From a young age, Loren was inspired by his father to honor and respect people with whom he worked, to work hard, and to be committed to sound business practices. Loren continues his father's legacy and he's doing it in his own way. Because Dick Baidas inspired his son by his life, when abruptly faced with his death, he already had a successor in place.

Inspiring your heirs doesn't always lead to a successor for your business. The son of Warren Buffett didn't become a big-time investor. He's a musician and he said, ". . . The silver spoon in the mouth too often becomes the silver dagger in the back—an ill-considered gift that saps ambition and drains motivation, that deprives a young person of the greatest adventure of finding his or her own way.

"The most important gifts of all had nothing to do with money. These were the gifts of parental love and close community and warm friendship, of inspiring teachers and mentors who took delight in our development. There were the mysterious gifts of talent and competence, capacity for empathy and hard work. These gifts were meant to be respected and repaid."[15]

You can't assume your heirs will understand your deepest feelings or know what you mean simply because they know you. It takes intentional and thoughtful planning as well as decisive action to build your pathway and to do it in such a way that you inspire your heirs to fulfill your wealth wishes and instructions.

For instance, you give to a nonprofit organization and perhaps have done it for years. You *assume* your family and heirs know what you're doing and also grasp your reasons so they'll carry on your giving after you're gone.

But will they?

Your responsibility is to make certain they understand exactly what you want them to do and catch your vision of why you want to do it.

Let's say you own several businesses and you assume your heirs know how to carry on what you started. "I established this before they were born," you might say about your children. "They've grown up around my business."

It's true they've grown up around the business.

---

[15] *Life Is What You Make It: Find Your Own Path to Fulfillment* by Peter Buffett, (New York: Harmony Books, 2010), p.4.

It may be true that they understand the business thoroughly.

Maybe not.

Don't assume, and you probably know the adage about assuming.

Be certain.

Wealth is far more than money and it's ultimately those aspects of wealth that inspire generations.

I've also heard heirs say, "My mom (or dad or both parents) worked hard and made a lot of money," and that seems the extent of their knowledge. There is a lack of depth in their statement because they're young and not involved in building the business.

Most of the time it's as if the heirs have no awareness of *what* their parents did or what made them successful. They don't know the motivation and reasons behind the hours, days, and years of hard work.

Part of your "wealth responsibility" is to set straight the thinking of your heirs on the major issues of your concerns.

Inspiring heirs involves telling (and even retelling) your story and allowing them to engage with you. I call this concept story building.[16] Invite them to become part of your ongoing story. They will know this is not only about you and your life, but about them as well. Give them a sense of ownership.

---

[16] Story building can be captured in an Enduring Wealth Family Letter of Intent.

Story Building
If I help my heirs understand me,
they can better understand themselves.

Open up and share your passions and goals and your life with the people you love. When you do, you help your heirs find their way in the world and empower them to find themselves. They also gain a better grasp of your story and their part in the story.

A good story covers all the aspects of who, what, when, where, why, and how. Building a no regrets wealth story uses those six questions, answers them, and brings to light the impact of those answers on subsequent generations.

Don't expect or assume they will do exactly what you're doing. But they will understand your intentions—your heart—because they have become part of your story. The purpose is not to impress them or prove how successful or wonderful you are. The purpose and outcome are to give them a stronger context for their lives and to honor the legacy of the family.

A proper inheritance-preparation strategy is guided by *how* you want to inspire your heirs.

First, your story can inspire them. Don't underestimate the power of your story. You are saying to them, "I have a context for my life."[17]

---

[17] The Family Wealth Letter of Intent offers a "generational inspiration" for the family.

As you explain who you are and open yourself to your heirs, it provides them with a context for their own lives. You empower them with your understanding of wealth and its meaning.

You're not just telling your story, you're helping the next generation tell their personal story as well.

Second, a planned inheritance can inspire heirs. There are reasons behind what you're doing. You've thought them through and your heirs deserve to be aware of your reasoning and what you decided.

Your plan can teach them responsibility, and express your confidence they will fulfill your final wishes. It also allows you to see what they do with it. You can react and adjust as necessary. A well-planned inheritance allows them to find themselves and affords the opportunity to pursue their own dreams.

Warren Buffett, the chairman of Berkshire Hathaway, believes the right amount of money to leave to children is "enough money so that they feel they could do anything, but not so much that they could do nothing."

Third, your charitable endeavors can inspire your heirs. They can learn to give back because they follow your example and see the meaning behind your giving. Giving back frees them to selflessly serve the world in whatever profession they choose.

For example, my father gave millions of dollars to church-building programs, youth camps, and even individuals. I admired his generosity. It was freeing once I understood that he hadn't intended for me to pay for church buildings, but only that I was to give generously to the causes I care about.

If you involve your heirs by acquainting them with the organizations and individuals to whom you give, and provide them with your rationale for giving, you can inspire them.

They can know what you wish to do with the funds, but perhaps even more important, they are able to understand the reason behind your generosity.

They will more fully understand what is important to you.

It may even surprise you how charitably minded the next generation can be. Inspired by your example, they may give even more to others and to causes that touch their hearts. They may be given more time than money but they are valuable resources.

All parents want their children to be happy. An inspired inheritance can encourage their well-being and give them a strong sense of having a purpose in life.

**Your goal isn't to impress them with how much
you have given or will give;
your role is to inspire the responsibility
of what to do with wealth.**

I was the heir apparent to my father's company, but I made the difficult decision in college to go my own way. I didn't take over the family business. Growing up, my father was my hero and in so many ways, I wanted to be just like him.

I've often thought if I can become only half the man he was, I'd be an incredible success and a tribute to him.

After college I realized the family business wasn't for me, and that was difficult for me to face. But his business held no serious interest for me.

I am entrepreneurial like my father; I also learned a big lesson from him about being generous toward others.

Consequently, I pursued nonprofit work and ventures for giving back to others that served them at their point of need. But had I not understood my father's story and myself, it would have been that much more difficult to put the pieces together about why I'm generous with time and money.

One priceless statement my father left me with before he passed away was, "Barry, always be a giver not a taker."

What Now?

1. Have you articulated your story for your heirs so they know how you created your wealth, how you've kept it, and the challenges you've overcome in life to get it?
2. Do your heirs understand your wealth story well enough so they can create their own stories within the context of your family's rich history?
3. What are you actively doing to help them understand and live their purpose? Does your planned inheritance support them in being able to carry it out?
4. What is one investment you could make in them in your lifetime that could propel them forward in life? How would making the investment feel to you? And would difference would that make for them?

Wealth With No Regrets planning is purposeful giving in your lifetime and beyond.

The sole purpose of being rich is to
give away money.
—Andrew Carnegie

12. Experience Purposeful Giving

In recent years, billionaires such as Warren Buffett and Bill Gates have urged successful people with an abundance of resources to give away 50 percent of their wealth.

They have figured out that the laws of our land require philanthropy. It can be voluntary or involuntary. The choice is yours to give it while you're living, or it will be given when you're gone.

How do you give with purpose in your lifetime?

I know a couple who figured that out. Fred and Millie Cargill, as I will refer to them, have been married 40 years. They both came from what we call "humble beginnings" and their families wanted them to receive an education beyond high school. There was one problem: Neither family had any money.

However, Fred and Millie received the education they wanted. They received it through the sacrificial giving of others. The gifts were indeed *sacrificial* because family members and friends, and even a few strangers, gave them money. The gifts came not from their excess, but out of their own poverty.

Fred and Millie both felt blessed by the opportunities given to them and the education they received. But they

95

found a greater purpose in their giving when it became connected to their story.

They now give scholarships to individuals to receive an education who otherwise would not be able to attend college. As a result, they are experiencing a new-found joy in their generosity.

Giving becomes purposeful when it's personal.

If you have purpose in your giving, you'll also discover joy and inner peace. You can make giving something you think through as thoroughly as you do a new business opportunity. A philanthropic venture would include questions such as:

- What is your level of joy in giving?
- Does your giving connect with your life story?
- What charities align with your story?

The approach you take is determined by your bias in giving. My mentor in estate planning, Jay Link, artfully articulated such approaches as being either a rifle or a shotgun approach. The difference is in giving smaller amounts to many charities, or in giving larger amounts to fewer charities.

Using a shotgun approach to giving $100,000, you might give to as many as 200 charities through $500 gifts. With a rifle approach you may give to as few as four charities through $25,000 gifts.

Which approach matches up with your desires and where do you believe you have the most impact from your gifts?

Will you be a voluntary or involuntary philanthropist?

When it comes to giving, the question is whether you choose to be charitable voluntarily or involuntarily. If you don't decide to give while you're alive, the government becomes your primary beneficiary after your death through mandatory estate taxes.

One way or another, you will be charitable.

Most affluent people don't know how to give strategically. That's not to say they're miserly or they don't want to give. It means they don't *understand* giving with a specific purpose, or how to do it in the most tax-efficient manner. For instance, my father didn't realize he could have given company stock instead of his income, which would have reduced his income taxes and increased his charitable giving.

This is like giving with wholesale dollars instead of retail dollars. Simply put, it is getting more bang for the buck.

Think about yourself. You focused heavily on earning your wealth, and now that you have it, you may not be sure what to do with it.

Give as much attention to the distribution of your wealth as you did in building it. Your wealth will be distributed by someone when you're gone. If you don't direct where it goes, it will most likely go in ways you didn't intend.

Are you giving as much attention to your wealth preservation and distribution as you did to wealth creation?

Surplus wealth is a sacred trust,
which its possessor is bound to administer
in his lifetime for the good of the community.
—Andrew Carnegie

Generosity is the cure for the disease of "affluenza."

R.G. Le Tourneau, the inventor of large earth-moving equipment, has inspired many, including my wife and me. Early in his career, and long before he made any significant amount of money, he determined to give away 90 percent of his income for the rest of his life.

Ninety percent!

After he became wealthy, he continued to keep only 10 percent of his income.

Someone once asked Le Tourneau, "How can you be so rich when you give away so much?"

"I shovel it out, and God shovels it back in," he answered, "and God has a bigger shovel."[18]

Regardless of your religious belief, there is a profound truth here to consider. Generosity has the power to help others and even to transform your own life.

---

[18] Go to www.boomfish.net/resources to preview R.G. Le Tourneau's book, *Mover of Men and Mountains.*

What Now?

1. Are you doing the kind of giving you want or would you like to do more?
2. Would you give more if you knew how to give assets and increase your tax advantages?
3. Do you and your spouse have a strategic philanthropic plan that represents what having wealth with no regrets means to you?
4. Do you ever wonder if you are holding back in your giving when you want to give more but don't know if you can and don't know how to do it?

Wealth With No Regrets planning is keeping control of wealth to meet your needs and goals.

O, it is excellent to have a giant's strength,
but it is tyrannous to use it like a giant.
—William Shakespeare

13. Control Your Wealth and Where It Goes

We want to believe we're in control of our world, don't we? There are certainly aspects of our lives we can control such as our attitude; there are things we can't control such as the attitudes and behavior of others.

When it comes to estate planning there are aspects you can control such as how and where to direct your wealth. All too often the wealthy choose not to take control of the direction of their wealth, just as they chose not to have the most beneficial attitude.

The third advantage of thorough wealth planning happens when you keep your heart at the center so you maintain control over what you own and where the assets go.

Control is often a derogatory word, but I want you to think of it as a positive concept. If you don't like that word, perhaps you prefer to say you have power or jurisdiction over your wealth or you can manage it.

Control results from understanding and using programs that fit your need. If, for instance, you want to manage your assets, but your plan asks you to give up control, you can do that.

If you decide and designate how you want your assets used, that's having control over your wealth. No one can change that written decision without your consent—which is a way to remind you that you have jurisdiction.

I want to be clear that if you have a business or assets, with the right tools, you can give up control and remain in charge of your wealth. You can allocate funds to your heirs and specify charities in an efficient way.

A good, well thought-out plan will help you take charge of the destiny of your wealth. For that to happen, however, you need to be educated about the impact your wealth has now and can have. You are thus empowered to decide what *you* want done with your assets.

Here's another approach. You make decisions for your wealth that are based on what you want to achieve for yourself. And why shouldn't you have that authority? You worked hard and persistently and you deserve to decide what happens to the things for which you struggled and sacrificed.

But first you have to let go of the way you do things now.

That sentence reminds me of something Avery Kate, my two-year-old daughter, did. After she dropped a pink golf ball into a vase, she reached inside to retrieve it. That was simple enough, but she had a problem. She gripped the ball and when she tried to pull it out, she couldn't. The ball inside her fist was too large to get through the opening.

Lori had to teach her that the only way to get the golf ball and her hand free was to let go of the ball first. Then she tipped the vase and the ball rolled out.

Avery Kate got what she wanted—the ball—but she had to learn a new way to make it happen.

Here are four things for you to consider in the matter of control.

First is the control of your assets while you fund inheritances. There are available tools that allow you to allocate money for those to whom you want to give. You can provide as much of your assets as you choose, even your business. If done correctly, you can still remain in control of the assets as long as you desire.

Second is control over your wealth story. A story will be told about you, your life, and what mattered most to you. If you don't tell this story, it will be interpreted from the bias of others' perspectives. Wouldn't you rather tell your own story and be sure it's what you want?

Third is control over your lifestyle. You built your wealth and in transitioning your business to the next generation or business partners, your lifestyle shouldn't depend on their decision making.

Fourth is control over your charitable giving. In cost-effective ways you give portions of your business, cash, and other assets without losing control over where they go. And you don't need to establish a private foundation to accomplish that. In fact, depending on your objectives, a private foundation could be the worst vehicle for staying in control of your charitable giving.

Suppose you aren't willing to relinquish the management of your business, mainly because you're not confident your son or daughter could run the business efficiently. In your mind, the business is linked to your retirement. No business, no retirement. If you died, no funds for your spouse.

Typically, ownership is linked to control. One of the fears in estate planning for business owners is giving up ownership of the business while the livelihood is dependent on the success of the business. For estate planning purposes, however, the estate-tax burden often can't be relieved until ownership passes. The wise thing to do is to pass on the ownership without giving up control.

Here's another true story. Harold Turner didn't understand the difference so he retained both control and ownership right up to his death. The business became a windfall for his oldest daughter, Sally, when she took over both ownership and control. She didn't understand how to operate the business or why he did it the way he did.

It took only three years for the business to no longer exist.

Here's the point: There are estate-planning tools and techniques that allow you to relinquish ownership for estate planning purposes, and yet retain control as long as you need or want it for your lifestyle and income. In doing that, you're also able to train the next generation to be owners. As you give, they learn.

Giving slowly to the heirs tests their character and ability and demonstrates your confidence in them. If the heirs manage the business and themselves as well, add to it.

That's the principle Dick Baidas used to groom his son Loren to take over the business. As Loren handled himself responsibly, he was promoted up through the company.[19]

For estate planning purposes, giving up ownership can open up a world of opportunity for you and your heirs. It's beneficial in helping to eliminate estate taxes and reduce capital gains and income taxes. Even more beneficial is the potential of what can happen in the relationships.

Take control of your estate planning by making necessary decisions now.

Give up ownership, but maintain control as long as needed.

Use the available planning techniques that help you accomplish these things.

---

[19] You can read the story in Chapter 11.

What Now?

1. Does your estate plan allow for maximum control, but minimum ownership allowing you to achieve the greatest leverage in planning with your assets?
2. What amount of ownership have you transferred to your heirs or charity to accomplish your wealth goals and objectives?
3. Do you have a plan that allows you to retain control of your assets for as long as you desire, or as long as your lifestyle is dependent on the profit from that asset?

Wealth With No Regrets
planning is creatively
accomplishing what you want.

If you have built castles in the air, your work need
not be lost; that is where they should be.
Now put the foundations under them.
—Henry David Thoreau

14. Implement a Creative and Actionable Plan

Wouldn't you like to be able to say yes to these questions?

1. Are my spouse and I living confidently with our wealth plan?
2. Am I inspiring my heirs with the inheritance I've planned?
3. Right now, am I giving with clear intent and purpose?
4. Does my wealth plan allow me control over the distribution of my assets?

If you've answered yes to all four, they prepare you to ask one more—perhaps the most important question:

How do I accomplish these four things?

If you've figured out the other parts, you're ready to move into what I call *creative planning.*

In achieving your level of success, you've frequently pushed the limits of your potential. Now you can push the limits with your wealth. I'm not implying the use of questionable tax practices that are unethical or unlawful, but the use of techniques allowed in the tax code.

Don't get comfortable with your plans as they are today.

Explore.

Get a second opinion of the possibilities available to you.

You can decide exactly what you want to do with your wealth. This can be creative as well as fulfilling. It can enable you to say to yourself with great joy and peace of mind, "This is my legacy."

You can succeed in every area of your life, but if you fail in your wealth planning, you risk your legacy being forever tarnished.

I hated to write those words because it forced me to think about my dad. His legacy is tarnished. It's not what Dad would have wanted.

Our situation—our confusion and heartache in particular—didn't represent the wise and humble, caring man he was. He didn't know there was another way to go about planning. He didn't know how to incorporate critical planning techniques to help him accomplish his goals.

If only my father had known, he wouldn't have allowed this mess.

That's why I'm so insistent that when you use the right techniques and implement a plan that represents *you,* the results are positive and powerful.

When it comes to creative planning, the first question you need to be able to answer with confidence is, "Do I have a zero-estate tax plan?

Regardless of the changing estate tax laws your answer can always be yes.

"The United States is the greatest asset protection country in the world," Bob Alexander, a prominent estate planning attorney, asserts, "but no one knows it."[20]

When you can answer affirmatively to the question, "Do I have a zero-estate plan?" you raise another question. "Is *creative* another word for unlawful or unethical?"

Certainly not.

The IRS tax code gives you the freedom to create a zero estate tax. Bob Alexander says, "Advanced planning techniques are audit proof."[21]

This point reminds me that I recently had the opportunity to ride in and then to drive a real NASCAR race car at the Atlanta Motor Speedway. For the first five laps around the track, I was a passenger with a seasoned race driver. Being from Detroit, I grew up around cars and speed, but this was more gripping and thrilling than I imagined.

As we entered each turn, I stiffened. At speeds up to 150 miles an hour, the car came within inches of hitting the outside wall. The professional driver smiled at how impressed I was with what the car could do.

Then it was my turn and he sat next to me. I didn't drive anywhere near his speed, but in my head was the potential of what I could work up to doing. I also realized that I didn't need all the speed he used for me to accomplish my objective of driving safely around the

---

[20] Mr. Alexander communicated this to an estate planning colleague of mine when they did planning for a client of his.
[21] Ibid.

track while experiencing the thrill of steering a NASCAR like the professionals.

I share this account to say: The tools for creating a zero-estate tax plan and reducing capital gains, and even lessening your income taxes, are available. You don't have to use them. You can get around, as I did on the track, without maximizing the potential of the engine.

But is simply getting around the track good enough for you? If you want the most benefits, you need a professional. You do that in much the same way the professional driver showed me how to drive the race car, although I couldn't do it nearly as well as he could.

You need someone who understands you and your capabilities and also knows how to use the resources to their maximum potential. You don't have to take advantage of the opportunity, but it's there. Creative planning allows you to seize the opportunities based on your objectives, and the assets that make up your estate.

You've worked hard for many years to make as much money as possible in your business. Having achieved your degree of success, I assume you also want to reduce the impact of taxes on your wealth.

Why would you hand over your hard-earned assets to the federal government when the law provides a way for you not to pay them? Unless you understand how the tax laws work, you'll give far, far more than you need to pay.

That makes it essential to incorporate creative planning techniques and strategies into your estate plan.

The secret to using the strategies is to have clear objectives that align with your heart and have emerged from your wealth story—the story about why you are who you are, how you came into the wealth you have, and what matters most to you about distributing your assets. Those goals and objectives need to be from your heart and not driven only by the planning tools and expensive techniques.

The tools and techniques should serve your objectives and not the other way around. That ensures the implementation of the creative planning strategies.

You can have the best techniques available to you, but if you don't have great clarity about where you want to go, you can get lost in the options available.

Even the greatest plan is meaningless without implementation.

The secret to creative planning and implementation includes:

- transparency about the challenges that concern you and the awareness of what you'd like to do;
- clear and numerically defined goals and objectives;
- open-mindedness about other ways to accomplish what you want to happen.

Use creative techniques that serve your goals, and implement your plan while you can see the fruit of your labor.

Don't wait!

What Now?
1. Do you have an estate plan that maximizes what you can give to heirs and charity?
2. Do you have an estate plan that uses planning techniques to allow maximum use of your wealth to accomplish your goals and objectives?
3. Do you ever wonder about what's in place and whether you're seizing every opportunity available to you?

Part 3:

Strategic Next Steps

Getting different results requires
doing the right planning
right now.

Wealth With No Regrets planning answers the three most important questions.

I try to give to the poor people for love
what the rich could get for money.
No, I wouldn't touch a leper for a thousand pounds;
yet I willingly cure him for the love of God.
—Mother Teresa

15. Three Important Questions You Need to Face

Norman Rockwell's painting "Freedom from Want" depicts a family gathered around the Thanksgiving dinner table expressing that they have enough for what they need. What strikes me is that the setting isn't elaborate. It's simple, relational, and cheerful.

This image sets the stage for three foundational planning questions. As you consider these questions, do so with the thought of what your Norman Rockwell "Freedom from Want" looks like for you.

1. How Much Is Enough for Me?

How much money do I need to keep for myself and my spouse to maintain our desired lifestyle?

How much is enough *for us*?

That may seem like a silly question. You can have just about anything in this world you want. There probably aren't many things you truly want and don't have.

If that's true, that makes the question even more crucial.

So here it is again: **How much is enough for me?**

There are two extreme answers to this question. One is, "I want to consume all I can on myself while I have the chance." Some individuals make that choice.

That leads to certain outcomes. One of them is what I call self-implosion as a result of self-consumption. Think of the actor Nicolas Cage. He is a box-office star, Academy Award winner, and earns millions of dollars.

He's also spent millions—more millions than he has earned. Here are a few documented items on which he spent his earnings:

- He paid eight million dollars for Mitford Castle in England and 17.5 million for his mansion in Bel Air, an expensive, residential suburb of Los Angeles.
- He became the owner of nine Rolls-Royces and other rare, expensive automobiles.
- He bought exotic animals.
- He purchased a Gulfstream Jet.
- He owns 30 motorcycles.
- He purchased a mega-yacht.
- He acquired an Enzo Ferrari—one of only 349 in the world, and the price was at least one million dollars.

The public record in November of 2009 says he *owed* 6.5 million dollars in unpaid back taxes. I mention Gage because he exemplifies one extreme response that says, "It's never enough for me."

The other extreme is to give away every penny right now. You survive your final years by living on the generosity of others.

How much is enough for me?

Years ago I read a short story by Leo Tolstoy called, "How Much Land Does a Man Need?"

As I remember it, God showed a man a vast stretch of land and said, "Every inch of land on which you step will be yours." There was only one condition: The man had to be back at the starting place at sundown.

The joyful man raced across the verdant fields, hurrying to claim as much land as possible. At high noon, he thought about turning back, but the land ahead looked better than anything he had yet seen. He pressed on.

By mid-afternoon, he realized it was getting late and he'd now have to run fast to get back by sunset. He started running. He reached the spot just as the sun set.

And he died on the spot.

"How much land does a man need?"

Tolstoy's answer: six feet by three—just enough to bury him.

I share this recognizing that money and even extreme amounts of money are neither bad nor wrong. My purpose is to paint an extreme picture of the reality of how much is ultimately needed for each person.

The wisdom of this can be found in these words: "People who boast of their wealth don't understand; they will die, just like animals."[22]

My mother, Yvonne, is nostalgic so memories of her upbringing are quite vivid and memorable. As a child and then a young adult living in Detroit, she always had barely enough for that day. By American standards, she

---

[22] Psalm 49:20.

was poor. But she didn't know it, and didn't consider herself impoverished. In her mind, she had everything she needed.

After she and my father made millions of dollars, she occasionally reminisced about those early days when she had to ride the bus to work because she couldn't afford a car. She recognizes that she and my father had more than enough even then. Having more would not have made them happier.

How much is enough for me?

When it comes to answering the question, it is probably less than you think.

What's the right answer for you? I don't know, but you do. Most likely, it is somewhere between the two extremes of never enough and giving away everything.

With every couple, no matter how rich, there is a numerical amount of money that matches the lifestyle they feel is appropriate for them to live. Most of the time they haven't thought much about a specific number or made a conscious decision to cap their lifestyle at that amount.

To consciously quantify the amount creates the opportunity to do serious planning that accomplishes your heart's deepest desires in life.

Another Wealth With No Regrets Secret:
Until you know how much you need, it's nearly
impossible to make decisions about
how much to give away.

Deciding how much is enough for you right now—and in the immediate future—opens up a world of planning opportunities. Deciding on *your standard of contentment* offers you the freedom to live and do the things in life that matter most to you.

2. How Much Is Enough for My Heirs?

Deciding on an inheritance for your heirs goes beyond having an answer to a percentage of the estate or even an exact dollar amount. There are several bigger questions to consider. For instance, does your plan encourage an attitude of gratitude? Or does it enable a sense of entitlement?

You also need to consider whether you want to fund opportunity or lifestyle. In answering these questions, be clear about whether you're enabling your heirs to pursue their passion and purpose.

For simplicity's sake, assume you have a net worth of 20 million dollars. You decide your two children should each receive half of the estate. We'll assume the assets are positioned in such a way that they can be divided in equal shares.

Let's also assume that it's a poorly planned estate that will cause an estate tax of 50 percent. So on the twenty-million dollar estate, ten million will go to estate taxes, leaving ten million to divide between your two heirs.

Your desire is for each child to be treated equally. Regardless of age, level of maturity, or phase of life you've settled on that plan.

With the help of your estate planner, you probably believe you've answered the inheritance question.

Is this enough?
Is it too much?
How much is enough?
Equal isn't always fair and fair isn't always equal.

The maturity of each child is critically important. Consider also the foresight or vision your children have. The inheritance should match the size of their ability to carry out their visions.

By *vision,* I mean the desire, purpose, or dreams of your children. They might want to start a business, begin a nonprofit organization, or change the world in some way instead of merely becoming part of the labor force.

Infusing the visionary children with a million dollars is different from doing the same thing with those who lack purpose or intention. Visionaries use their inheritance to make more or to leverage it to help others in a way greater than they could without it. Or the money helps heirs get the businesses going quicker and smoother without the burden of heavy debt.

You also need to consider your children's ability to carry out their intended vision. What about their responsibility to manage their dreams after they've become functional?

Those are a few of the important factors for you to consider beyond a dollar amount and a certain age to pass it on. That's the traditional approach.

**How much is enough for your heirs?
Does the amount benefit and inspire them?**

Back to our analogy of deciding on the right amount of inheritance.

- You've settled the amount of five million dollars for each child.
- Your estate has the assets to accomplish what you want to do.
- You've finished the inheritance discussion.

Or not.

Let's play out the situation.

Let's say one child is 30 years old, married, and has two children. She and her husband earn $130,000 dollars a year. In a windfall moment, you will infuse her lifestyle with five million dollars.

Conservatively, if she invests all the inherited money, taking only the income off the investment at five percent a year, that inheritance will produce more than twice the gross household income to which she's accustomed.

So far so good.

Assuming you understand this and have the appropriate documents drafted properly, you will have accomplished what you set out to do.

Here are your sub-questions:

- Did you help or hurt her?
- Do you consider this a lifestyle or opportunity inheritance?
- Do you know her spouse well enough to understand how this will affect him?
- Is she responsible enough to handle that much income?

- Is she mature enough to maintain her course in life?
- Is it good or bad to infuse a lifestyle with $250,000 of additional tax-free income?

I don't know the answer, but you need to think through the implications of the bequest.

Most parents rarely do. They feel perplexed about what to do with a financial legacy for their heirs. And how do they arrive at the right answer?

Let's say your other child, a son, is 24 years old and hasn't yet found his way. He earns about $15,000 a year doing odd jobs. Since you treated each child equally, you've infused his lifestyle with more than *sixteen times* the income to which he is accustomed.

Now ask those same six questions as you did for your daughter.

As the above illustration demonstrates, you now have to face new questions:

Is the right amount of inheritance
the total of your surplus beyond what you need,
or only a portion of it?

A common mistake is to leave an inheritance at the end of your life. Why not begin giving it during your lifetime so you can see the effect it has on your beneficiaries?

You can't resolve this dilemma without well thought-out answers. It requires thorough thinking, asking the right questions, detailed analysis, and time to consider your options.

The more thoughtful, thorough, and informed your decisions are about the inheritance issue, the greater the probability that the financial legacy will serve the purpose you intend.

Let's assume that the ultimate purpose is for your children to be happy.

- Will more money make them happier?
- Will a surprise windfall event at the end of your life make them happier?
- Will knowing how much you intend to leave them help you discern whether the planned inheritance will contribute to their happiness?
- Will giving some portion of the inheritance now while you're able to see the results help you to make decisions about the impact of their inheritance on their happiness?

Make informed decisions about the inheritance of your heirs.

Don't allow standard estate-planning procedures to make the decisions for you.

Another benefit of planning bequests early is the opportunity to communicate the intent, amount, and timing behind the inheritance. A family meeting about wealth and the purpose behind a financial legacy can pay huge dividends in helping heirs remain resolute about discovering and living their purpose in life.

For instance, too often yearly gift checks are handed out to heirs without any explanation or understanding. Over time the heirs expect those checks—as though they deserve it. They often build a lifestyle around the assurance of those regular gifts.

The questions for you are whether you're accomplishing your desired intent with the money.

- Will you be funding an inflated lifestyle or an opportunity?
- Are you encouraging an attitude of gratitude or entitlement?
- Are they being responsible and sensible with the funds?
- Will they willingly report to you about what they did with it?
- What do you hope they will do with the money?

3. How Much Is Enough for Others?
The third question is about the impact you desire to have on others beyond your heirs.

- To whom do you want your charitable dollars to go?
- Do you want to give funds to an organization, church, synagogue, or charity?
- If so, how much do you want to give?

As discussed in Chapter 12, knowing, articulating, and writing your story helps answer these important questions.

As of 2013, your Uncle Sam has determined that you will be charitable to as much as 50 percent of your estate. The question isn't whether you're charitable or not. The question is: Do you want to be charitable voluntarily or involuntarily? If you don't make voluntary charitable giving part of your wealth plan, Uncle Sam will be sure it is after you're gone. It's called gift and estate taxes.

The great news is this: You have a choice.

If you choose voluntary charity, there are enormous options available to you. The options include tax elimination, and even more significant, you can experience great joy in deciding how to help others.

Let's go back to the earlier example of the twenty-million dollar estate where half of the money was paid to the government in estate taxes. If you do your planning correctly and incorporate voluntary philanthropy into it, you can disinherit the IRS completely, and at the same time, increase the inheritance to your heirs.

Voluntary philanthropy allows you to begin giving right now the 10 million dollars that would have gone to the IRS and you can still provide 10 million to your heirs.

Those are three all-important questions that need to be worked through carefully. Wisdom beckons you to not ignore them, but to start planning so that *your wishes* will prevail now and after you're gone.

What Now?

1. Have you and your spouse determined how much you will need to live on as you age?
2. Have you established a plan that gives you confidence that you will not outlive your money?
3. Have you and your spouse had detailed conversations about the purpose and impact of your planned inheritance on our heirs?
4. Have your and your spouse discussed the important people and charities, and how your wealth will be bestowed in such a way as to benefit society for the greater good?

Wealth With No Regrets gets the help of specialists to accomplish goals and objectives that matter.

Don't let what you cannot do interfere
with what you can do.
—Coach John Wooden

16. What Now?

What do you do with the information presented in this book?

Do you stick the book on a shelf and in the back of your mind promise yourself you'll get around to it one day?

You could do that.

But please, please don't.

The day for action is right now. Today.

Don't wait.

The enemy to tax-efficient estate planning is not the IRS, but procrastination.

As the saying goes, "You have only today, you aren't guaranteed tomorrow."

Tomorrow may seem a long way into the future.

And perhaps it is.

Or maybe not.

A few weeks ago a close friend received the horrifying news that none of us wants to hear: "There is nothing else we can do for you."

These were the words of his oncologist after reviewing the latest scans of his body. The cancer had returned and was spreading rapidly.

As I'm doing the final edits on this book, my friend is no longer with us on earth. He was 40 years old and father of two children, ages five and two.

He *knew* his days were limited but they were even fewer than he had been told. All our days are limited, but too many of us need a medical diagnosis to accept that reality.

You can learn to live with a sense of destiny and purpose. That way, whether the end is soon or a decade away, you'll be ready.

Live by taking action now.

Carpe Diem. Seize the day.

If anything written in this book nudged you, even a little, take action.

Don't wait. You may not be given tomorrow.

If you already have an estate plan, I recommend getting a second opinion from an independent, objective advisor who can guide you about fulfilling the desires of your heart—someone who understands the available planning techniques and can also put them in language you can understand and help you put your plan into action.

Don't wait.

The success of effective wealth planning is to keep your heart at the center of your planning, and allow your head to come into agreement with the desires of your heart.

Can you name a professional athlete who has been successful as a professional in two sports?

Maybe you can name one or two, and the first person that comes to my mind is Bo Jackson. Next to come to the surface is Deon Sanders, who excelled as a cornerback in football and as an outfielder in baseball.

Try to name a professional athlete who failed to excel as a professional at two sports.

I immediately think of one of the greatest athletes of all time, Michael Jordan. Basketball was his gift, and it was magic to watch him on the court. But when it came to applying his competitive advantage and skill to baseball, it just didn't work out as well.

You, too, are a professional in your area of expertise.

It is unlikely that you are also a professional in the area of wealth planning.

One ultra-affluent man, whom I'll call Jacob, entrusted his wealth planning to his reputable estate-planning attorney and it resulted in a $26 million dollar estate tax on his $50 plus million dollar estate.

Unless you want to be like Jacob, you need a professional to help you with your planning. The process should allow you to express your deepest desires and give you clear direction about where you're going and how to get there.

You want a specialist to help you put this area of your life—your wealth—together for you. You need someone who can take you where you want to go and give you the kind of experience that's personal and competent in all the issues.

I've often heard successful people say, "I wish someone could help me think through my wealth planning without trying to sell me something."

Can you relate to that sentiment?

No group is more targeted by product sales people than the affluent. It's as if you wear a sign on your chest that says, "Please try to sell me something."

The ultimate agenda of the product sales personnel is to sell the product on which they'll receive the greatest commission, or a product that elevates them to a higher level within their organization.

Having grown up in the home of an affluent entrepreneur, I saw that firsthand. The approach becomes even more evident when looking for estate-planning help.

Many advisors position themselves by claiming to hold the silver bullet that will solve all your problems.

They make it sound easy; they make it sound simple.

It's neither.

The area of estate planning for the affluent is complicated, and it requires more than a one-size-fits-all answer to the challenges involved.

To do wealth planning right, you need a specialist, someone who focuses on you (on your heart), remains objective, understands the strategic and tactical, and is a team player who helps you make your plan happen.

A Specialist Focuses on You and
Your Particular Situation

Here are three things I want to point out about finding a specialist who is right for you and your situation.

1. The best way to determine if an advisor focuses on you and your situation is to spend face-to-face time with the person. How much time are you able to talk, as opposed to how much the advisor talks? If you're doing most of the listening, this obviously doesn't become *your* estate plan.

2. When an advisor talks, does the person help you think through your situation, dreams, and concerns? Or does the advisor continually talk about what he or she will do for you? A true specialist focuses on getting to know you and learning what's important and urgent about your situation.

3. A specialist should have a unique process that you can understand. This kind of advisor should speak in plain language, without using jargon that makes him or her appear superior.

A Specialist Remains Independent in Serving You

What you need is a person who can *independently* assess your situation by asking the right questions that draw out the desires of your heart. That way you can pursue opportunities and overcome the challenges that trouble you.

A true and honest specialist doesn't have a conflict of interest. His or her purpose is to serve you.

Here's an example of a woman who was worth several million dollars. Her desire was to give as much as possible to her heirs and to charity while she was alive. The plan to accomplish this meant the dwindling of principle during her lifetime.

An independent advisor would be open to designing this type of plan. If her advisor had been compensated by assets he had under management, it would have been difficult (perhaps impossible) to enact that kind of plan.

To remain independent, a specialist will charge a fee based on what the affluent family wants to accomplish and the complexity involved in making it happen.

The fee should be clearly understood and **based on clear wealth-planning outcomes of a defined and proven process.**

A Specialist Understands the Strategic Planning Tools

A typical session with an estate planner using a traditional approach will be about planning techniques for which the planner is familiar. The conversation unfolds where the advisor looks smart because he talks extensively about advanced planning by using names you can't pronounce.

A true specialist, however, captures the strategic opportunities available to you by helping you express your deepest desires. Because of technical expertise about what's available, a specialist is able to have a plain, candid conversation with you about the tactics needed to accomplish what you want to do with all your wealth.

The magic in wealth planning is in bringing the strategic desires of the family together with the techniques that apply.

All too often the planning tools drive the planning process, and too often don't produce the desired outcomes.

A Specialist Is a Team Player on Your Team

How often do your attorney, accountant, investment advisor, and business manager speak with one another? Do they even know one another's names?

A specialist should demonstrate the uniqueness of his or her process, clearly showing how it will bring out the expertise of all the advisers in a collaborative effort.

A specialist will probably deliver a method different from what your other trusted advisors suggest.

A specialist can coordinate and bring out the best in your trusted advisors to accomplish your unique desires. There is no competition between the specialist and other advisors because the specialist serves as the general contractor over the design and build of your wealth with no regrets envisioned future.

You Need a Specialist in Affluent Wealth Planning

If your family physician says you have heart disease and you take the medicine he prescribes but still have symptoms, what will you do? Are you going to go back to the same doctor? How many times will you go to the same person while you continue to have the same symptoms?

If you're told you need heart surgery, or even a heart transplant, won't you seek out a specialist? When my dad was told he needed a heart transplant we sought for the best surgeon in that specialty.

In wealth planning, when you still have concerns, including but not limited to estate taxes that will be due, and uncertainty about the preparation of your heirs, what are you going to do?

Wealth planning **is** a life-and-death issue.

My father invested his life into building his empire, and it was a serious investment of his time and resources. But he viewed estate planning as a cost and not an investment. For him it was also a burden he didn't want to deal with. He didn't deserve the outcomes we experienced as a result of his planning. He was a much better man than the results he received. He missed having a specialist who could bring all the pieces together for him.

Seek out a specialist who can deliver a unique process to give you the greatest probability for successful wealth planning and transfer.

Dedication

Dedicated to my family that includes the love of my life, Lori, and my son, Hudson, and daughter, Avery Kate. They are the most precious blessings from God, and the pinnacle of wealth in my life.

This book is also written in tribute to my late father, Dale H Spencer, who inspired me to live with purpose and meaning, always focused on giving back to others, and to my mother, Yvonne Spencer, for her inspiration and encouragement to always go for it.

I also dedicate this to my friend Matt, who lost his battle with cancer as I was completing this book. He was an inspiration to me, and left behind his wife and two young children.

Acknowledgments

This work came together with the help of a host of people. Those who helped me are passionate about No Regrets Wealth and the lasting quality and legacy of relationships. Their contribution has been many fold, including offering stories, examples, insights, editing, proofing, revising, and encouraging me.

First, thanks to my business partner, Scott Noble, and his wife, Denise, for their tireless effort in helping me focus ideas for this book, even before there was a title for it. They offered constructive criticism and insights into perceptions of readers and how to reword sections of the book for accuracy and clarity. They are also dear friends and one with me in heart about the importance of living Wealth With No Regrets.

Second, my thanks to many others who offered suggestions, input, and edits, and most of all gave encouragement to me in starting and completing the book. These people include, Craig and Kristen Butler, Pete and Debbie Fujimoto, Zollie and Valorie Maynard, Zollie and Jaime Maynard, Matt and Shawn Shorrock, and Loren and Sarah Baidas.

Many others have contributed to this work in their support of me personally over the years. These people include: Wally Armstrong, Ruth Baidas, Travis and Julianne Baxter, Roger Birkman, John and Marlene Boll, Ron Braund, Mark and Candi Brown, Vernon and Sandy Buchanan, Greg and Michelle Bushey, Alex and Chris Cann, Joey and Jennifer Carlton, Ed Chaffin, Keith and

143

Sondra Crutcher, Rich DeVoss, Carl Drury, Jim Exley, Mark and Dianee Fonseca, MaxPaul Franklin, Jerry and Jan Geiger, Matt and Tasha Given, Bryan Green, Stephanie Hamlin, Jim Hancock, Ron and Jan Hembree, Jane Hubbard, Jeff and Alicia Hylton, Andy and Diana Istvan, Todd and Sheri Jackson, Deane Johnson, Paul Johnson, Clyde and Cora Jones, Dee and Kay Kelley, Seldon and Nona Kelley, Scott Keffer, Justin and Bethany Knight, Mike and Judy Landry, Dave and Carol Lewis, Vernon and Carolyn Lunn, Tim and Valerie Marks, Dave Mason, Hugh Maclellan, Todd and Amy McClellan, Glenn and Chrysan McCoin, Mark and Amanda Mountain, Dean Nelson, Leslie and Lora Lee Parrott, Richard Parrott, John and Cissy Persichetti, Jim and Marge Petersen, Tim Philpot, Jim and Emily Pilat, Craig and Sue Pitters, Jack Pledger, Erich Ramsey, Dick Riddle, Ike Reighard, Rich and Grace Roles, Tom and Nancy Rost, Mike and Shannon Sapp, Tom and Rosemary Sechrist, Doc and Sharon Sloan, Michael and Amy Smalley, Shawn and Donna Spencer, Dave and Anne Stoddard, Deane and Beverly Stokes, Shirley Snyder, David Sveen, Bob and Sally Tamasy, Brad and Christine Thomas, Dani Weaver, David and Nancy White, Mark Whitmire, and Ken and Ginny Whitten.

Many thanks to Jay Link, founder and visionary of the Family Wealth Counseling movement, who provided extensive training to me from his 30 years of estate planning experience with affluent families. I'm indebted to Jay for his insights and wisdom about doing planning right. I thank the classmates I attended training sessions with as they shared their lives and stories—which also encouraged me to write this book.

Thanks to my mom, Yvonne, who encouraged me to write this book and tell our family experience with my father's estate. She not only believes in me, but also the hopeful message that I've communicated, wishing every family experience Wealth With No Regrets.

Last and most important, I want to thank my wife, Lori, without whom there would be no book. She encouraged me and kept the passion burning inside me to tell my story, and refocused my attention on the numbers of people that would be helped by my experiences and learning. She truly deserves all the accolades for this work, and for enduring the challenge of being married to me while living as an entrepreneur and taking on this project.

Ultimately, I thank my Heavenly Father for showing me love in His Son, Jesus Christ, who not only is my hope, but also the giver of all my talents and abilities. I'm a blessed man to experience His grace on a daily basis.

And thanks to you, the readers for investing your valuable time to read these pages. I trust it will prove to be a great benefit and lead you toward a life of wealth with no regrets.

Dale H Spencer   **Dale and Barry**

Contact the Author

Barry H Spencer

12600 Deerfield Parkway, Suite 100

Alpharetta, GA 30004

888-793-8332

barry@barryhspencer.com

www.WealthWithNoRegrets.com

www.TheSecretofWealthWithNoRegrets.com

EASY-ORDER INFORMATION

To receive the complimentary Special Report on, "The 7 Regrets Wealth Creates"

www.WealthWithNoRegrets.com

For additional copies of this book, complete the following form, call or fax the following information:

☐ Email barry@barryhspencer.com
☐ Phone in the following information: 888-793-8332.

I, _____ would like to receive
☐ ___number of copies (special pricing bulk pricing)

There is a 100 percent satisfaction guarantee. If not satisfied, you may return all items for a full refund.

Name _____

Address _____

City _____ State _____

Zip _____

Email _____

☐ MC ☐ VISA ☐ AMEX

CC # _____

EXP _____ 3/4 Digit Code _____

Signature _____

Barry Spencer is an entrepreneur, author, keynote speaker and creator of *Wealth With No Regrets®.* The *Wealth With No Regrets®* process is a highly relational and in-depth process that shows highly successful entrepreneurs, executives and woman who are on their own, how to enjoy their wealth more fully and avoid regrets in an easy to understand way by,

Clarifying and designing a bigger desirable future.

Identifying and removing obstacles that stand in the way.

Creating an accurate picture of the present wealth situation.

Building a bridge to the desired future for the family and causes that matter deeply.

Barry is passionate about his mission to motivate a billion dollars in generosity to family and causes without causing regrets.

Barry has had the unique opportunity to personally meet with leaders from coast to coast in the United States with a net worth up to a billion dollars asking them deeper questions about the challenges wealth has created for them and their family. He shares many of these insights in the special report, "The 7 Regrets Wealth Creates, and How To Avoid Them", and book, *From the Roots of Wealth Regrets to the Routs of No Regrets.*

For more information or the latest research Barry Spencer and his team are doing go to, www.WealthWithNoRegrets.com or call, 678-278-9632 and email, barry@barryhspencer.com.